Mule

Joan Cofrancesco

authorHOUSE®

AuthorHouse™
1663 Liberty Drive
Bloomington, IN 47403
www.authorhouse.com
Phone: 1 (800) 839-8640

Cover painting by Janine Bartolotti

Published by AuthorHouse 09/13/2017

ISBN: 978-1-5462-0895-2 (sc)
ISBN: 978-1-5462-0896-9 (e)

Print information available on the last page.

This book is printed on acid-free paper.

walking the erie
thinking of the mules

turtle meditates
on rock at erie canal
then plunges in mud

dead carp

dog days of august
a dead erie canal carp
licked by a stray cat

found poem
from the
diary of rachel wilmer 1830

6,800 horses
3,300 boats
85 locks
1 passenger
was taken
with
cholera

mule-drawn boats
once wending their way thru
the scenic countryside

syracuse once looked
like venice with its canals
bridges, boats, and aqueducts

sheets hang
on the line
my dog jumps
into the fed ex truck
again
we drink wine
another day
in the salt city

construction workers
boatmen and immigrants came
creating cities, towns and villages

erie canal

locks, aqueducts, mules
dewitt clinton had a dream
albany to buffalo

canallers rode on
wooden barges pulled by mules
363 miles

fallen leaves along
the erie canal path
boy in red sneakers

.

bridges, aqueducts and locks
a marvel of engineering
the erie canal

kayaking down the erie canal

paddling down the canal
i think of dewitt clinton
visionary

HIKING THROUGH THE ERIE
CANAL ON A PERFECT DAY

1.
wearing a beret with a kangaroo on the front
i walk out into leaves

look over a collection of crocks
put up by the erie canal museum,

watch a turtle plunge off
a huge rock.

2.
woke up at 6 a.m.
searched the refrigerator
drank apple cider
sucked a ripe plum.

3.
walking along the trail again
the orange and red leaves in red decay
sitting in the sun my 61-year-old friend,
his cane beside him watches geese.
i'm walking
half the sky turquoise
the other squirrel gray clouds
upper part of the canal brimming with sunlight.
i in my ripped jeans, flannel shirt
the 61-year-old wearing the same
under a white jacket.

in the bag there are some extra
apples, bread, grapes.

4.
do i-ching
write words
on rice paper
with new fountain pen,
eat chicken + rice—

perfect.

poem written after cross-country
skiing at the erie canal

sprawled out
on the floor
beside the woodstove
scribbling poems
listening to dawg's mandolin
camels on the floor
beside the cat
skis in the corner
glad to be alive

holstein staring at me
out of state fair barn
wish i could swish my tail
at these flies

i'm all about
woodsmoke
a walk along the erie canal
a cat beside me
a book of poetry by rilke
a glass of merlot
i'm all about
poetry and art
and a good
blues song
by janis
i'm all about
simplicity

magic

i see cats and frogs
along the trail—
friends who now
live in bogs

why you should adopt a canal cat

1. they don't argue.
2. they don't ask for money.
3. they don't stay out
   until 2AM then lie to you
   about where they've been.
4. they sleep with you
   no matter what.
5. they listen to vivaldi.
6. they don't talk in their sleep.
7. they let you write poems about them
   without explanation.

in 1870
clinton square
erie canal frozen
for ice skaters

humming the song
"mule named sal"
as i walk along
the camillus towpath
wondering
what it was like
to have lived back then

i dip my paddle
into the canal
look into the woods
see a deer
leap into
the september light

no need for a radio

driving to the canal
in an open green jeep
tree frogs create surround sound

erie canal animal haiku

geese chipmunks snakes fish
squirrels tree frogs turtles herrings
people walking their dogs

at 15

sunday at the canal
this was my religion—nature
and heaven was
riding my bike along the path
right out of town

those were the days:
mules
canal boats
praying to the holy ghost
homemade beer
cholera

i hear tree frogs
as i walk the path

multi colored leaves
dance on the wind

the skeleton of a deer
picked clean by crows

midnight

black canal cat stalks
chipmunks, birds, mice, grasshoppers
drinks from the canal

a black cat
leaps
into
the darkness
and the darkness
disappears

it's spring
basho's frogs
are diving ecstatically
off their logs
into the murky waters
of the erie canal

walking erie canal trail
the large golden retriever
shaking off the canal

kittens asleep in woodpile
gods asleep in temples

autumn at the canal

stray cat
november chill
cat tails

autumn leaves
yellow green red orange crimson gold
flying all over the path

stop along the path
to scribble in a small pad
a poem about frogs

a cyclist pedals
in the breeze
his wet tight shirt
clinging to his body

early sunny afternoon
happy dogs along the path
i'm in the dharma-realm

ravel's bolero
listening to my i-pod
my pace picks up

camillus erie canal

the damp smell of dirt
snapping turtles and black snakes
i try to avoid

poem to raymond carver

it's not basho's frog
or buson's frog
or bly's frog
it's finally my frog
but let's face it raymond
it is just
a frog

alone
writing poetry
by candlelight—
turtle season

the inner life

i'm going along fine
studying meditating
walking along the erie canal
then i drift back to earth
where you lay naked on my bed
pulled down
by your love
only a few scattered poems remain
of those ecstatic moments
between the pain suffering fights
lying naked beside you
red cliffs   martha's vineyard
thrashing sex
all night in
the adirondacks
dogs
howling outside

their spirits are there
native voices echoing
onondaga lake

in 1917
   picasso was
      inspired
         in naples
            by lysippus's statue
               of hercules

in 1971
   i was
      inspired
         in syracuse
            by you

waking up in upstate, new york
with someone i'm afraid to love
because you hurt me so badly

"And so the world
chilled, and the women wept, tore at their hair.
Yet, in the skies, a goddess governed Sirius, the Dog,
who shines alike on mothers, lesbians, and whores."
                    --A PASTICHE FOR EVE
                    Weldon Kees

wake me gently
from the first cold sheets
of november,
when logs have been smouldering
half the night while we were
making love
and thinking about that dogon star sirius
57,000,000,000,000 miles away.

our life is our art

sometimes you talk as if lennon
were still alive.
his photo taped to your refrigerator
shaved fish coming out of your speakers.
it is a cold december in syracuse
i sit by the fire reading tolstoy,
writing poetry,
picturing you in wire-rimmed glasses and faded jeans
playing guitar
still caught in the revolution
of the sixties.
out of love, comrade,
woman like myself in art and consciousness, sister
in whose notes rise and lower
inherently, my hope.

come
to syracuse
go to
7-rays bookstore
buy TANTRIC
SEX
sleep with me

above syracuse
nimo's spirit of light flies
giving us power

pulling the house around me
like an old afghan

because the winter days are short
i will sleep throughout this morning
light a single candle
pull the first cold sheets of december
over my head

this is where i jump-start my life stealing
dreams from bukowski's cats
who come in to sit by the flame—
three pairs of green eyes staring

L.L. bean night in syracuse

cold december night
i pull up my flannel sheets
reach for your warm ass

fate

flipping
through a self-help book
in barnes & noble

saw you
reading a collection
of japanese death poems

"You know what these
Syracuse winters are like
everyone becoming their
cat and on top of that
the pipes freeze."
                    Arielle Greenberg

come lie next to me
it's snowing outside and
there's nothing else to do

white out in syracuse

woodstove stuffed with applewood
candles lit on the tub
waves of bubbles washing over us
no houses or people in sight

poem to raymond carver

comforter thrown
over my legs
late morning
cats asleep at my feet
i am reading a tattered copy
of A NEW PATH TO THE WATERFALL
you said you wanted this
all of your life
waking each day to
everything new
choosing whether to
fish or write or play
with your cat morris.
i look outside at the new snow—
the same syracuse snow
that you must have watched
and i too feel like
lobotomizing the morning
rising only to cook brook trout
for breakfast.

january in upstate, new york

the snowflakes hang
in the air like small cat tongues
my cat asleep
by the woodstove

vivaldi's *four seasons*
for the anniversary of bukowski's death
and my almanac
already open for spring

suddenly we don't talk about the cold
as if it is lost forever, and you,

you my love, how do you say
your new mediterranean word,
how do you say
amore
with your italian passion
your black jockey briefs
still in place.

waking up in syracuse

saturday morning
on my apple computer
hangs your black frederick's bra

passion

radiator banging
chipmunks racing
through the walls
neighbor's stereo blasting
music to love you by

tradition

christmas eve
snow falls like
fat white cats
i wait for my mother's calamari

lazy winter day
nothing to write about in my journal
cats asleep by the fire

syracuse tanka

the cats are asleep
mozart on the stereo
snowflakes are falling
i am cuddling with you
on the big bed we just bought

another tanka

light
slowly filling the gutters
we are together
in front of the fireplace
drinking your dry chardonnay

dickens

empty old factories, dirty snow
i feel like a vagabond
marcellus casket company

gothic cathedral
13 sheep
24 hungry ghosts
another sleepless night

st. francis comes
to me
takes my cat
smoky
and walks
out the door
with him
under his arm

to saint francis

hey, fran
i've thrown away everything
except
a knapsack
crammed with my poems—
what do you think,

can i keep it?

temple bell
windowful of cats
i have been practicing
out of body travel
floating above your bed

spring in syracuse
i'm the runner-up again

alone
writing poetry
by candlelight
turtle season—
crawling back on logs
into this world

writing poetry
one cat and me,
drinking sake
midnight, june 1st.

i am intoxicated
by spring
and the smell of lilacs
you walk with me
at night
through the streets
of syracuse
always through
the streets of syracuse

dinosaur barbeque

my dog stops to sniff
between motorcycle spokes
a dinosaur bone

gold's gym

he wore a tomcat t-shirt
as he prowled around the gym
there was something about him
that i liked
his nike sneakers and perfect
butt
his tight black shorts
the way he would strut
over to the weights
like a muscular black panther

fat cat

wandering around alone
on wescott st. at 5:00 a.m.
purring because
you are asleep in my bed

syracuse

driving the north side
5 urban bathtub marys
on well mowed front lawns

a woman spreads her legs
sunset over onondaga lake
is boring

seven rays bookstore
tarot reading
hermit
death
fool
so what
else is new?

naked and muscular
moving through
the morning light
my lover brings me
blackberries
for breakfast

park bench

on a park bench on a syracuse night
with a dog and cup of vanilla
coffee
we watched lights off the parkway
after a poetry reading
with you striding beside me
we wandered
beneath streetlights
we passed dark houses
three barking dogs
two squirrels
we discussed rimbaud
in the moonlight
haunted by the ghost of the drunken poet
i carry my inspiration
from old abbeys
to dark bars
afternoon drifts into evening
i hid your souvenirs and prophecies
in tattered poetry books
i still think of you as i sit alone
on a dark green bench in onondaga parkway.

suny upstate medical center
august 9th, 2005

call in sick
stay in bed
all day reading
bukowski

living dead

we are
the living dead
we go to work
watch tv
go to bed
dressed in red
sex
our only joy

halloween

halloween
gorillas drive past
in blue volkswagens

trick or treat

my daughter asks me
if she can wear my hippie
bellbottoms and peace sign

octoberfest
beer polka beer
accordians, more beer

i'm simplifying my life

first there were the house,
the cat,
and you
soon i needed candles
bells
cushions
incense
meditation
then i got rid of the house,
the cat,
and you

aching muscles
from paddling
eager to return
home to a fire
and meows

sometimes its good
to be anonymous—
a cup of oolong tea
a mourning dove
a small book of poetry

ghosts under ice
at the erie canal
bass cooking in bordeaux

upstate ny winters
colorful bulky sweaters

at green lakes state park
my dog catches a frisbee
high above the lake

i stroll along
the tow path
of the erie canal
accompanied by
a watersnake

watching a cat
watching a
muskrat
at the
erie canal—
sex and death

a simple life
with books
cats a small garden

hot summer day
erie canal
the mouth of a carp
on the bank
opening
and closing

canal
geese fish
ass up

ny winter coming

in my old leather jacket
with a cup of sake
by a woodstove
i'm a goose
flying 1500 miles
south

poem to dlugos

slipping thru
the syracuse streets
i wish i owned
a pair of uggs
with fur inside
or that i was
in bed again with sue smith

poem to barry difford

evening, syracuse—
        woman in the window
leaning on the ridge, inhaling
        a joint
    she remembers
                janis joplin
    3 flights up
heavy, high
    exhaling pain
into
    the summer night

lighting the tree
in hanover square
six hundred colored bulbs—
i think of medieval monks
laboring in the monastery
on the illuminated manuscripts

italia fest
beer
dancing
beer
accordions
more dancing
more beer

at the dinosaur barbeque
a biker named jesus
drinking wine

syracuse snowstorm
how far
the dog star sirius
is from earth

i rake leaves
my orange cat watches
from the window

in syracuse
poetry is usually
the only way
to get to
a summer beach

i hunger for the big stuff—
you
and my cat
sitting beside me
in front of the fireplace
on a cold
syracuse night

the snow in a chinese poem
is not like the snow
in syracuse, ny
something you brush off
your car

camillus towpath
volunteers splitting wood
a chill in the air

syracuse
wires cross the blue spruces
chipmunks and cat
round and round
the steady rain

crows land
on the
no trespassing sign

syracuse sunday
the herald covered with snow
three crows on the line

walking home from school
chestnuts
in my front pocket

casino lights in
the cornfields onondagas
are getting even

cries of geese
light snow on the spruce
almost winter

i dip my paddle
into the canal
look into the woods
see a deer
leap into
the september light

chopping firewood
i can't wait
for the first snow

black harleys
and people sipping
beer outside
the dinosaur barbeque

skiing song mountain
snow white like mallarme's swan
syracuse winter

december
pine needles
and snow
in the cat's fur

i can still see her
liz cotton playing "freight train"
guitar upside down

winter night
frozen windchimes
on the porch

the sunday morning
3 crows on the
telephone line
syracuse-herald
covered with snow
loneliness

fest jazz
bouncing off
the sidewalks
reaching for the sky
to hold huge
puppets

autumn
upstate ny
watching cows
from my tub

your skin tastes like
apples
woodsmoke
maple syrup
upstate ny

7 days of snow
beethovan
woodstove cat
and you

goats beard
black steel
ice
powerlines
snowbanks
whiskey and walleyes
upstate new york

Printed in the United States
By Bookmasters